The Library

Julie Murray

Abdo
Kids

MY COMMUNITY: PLACES

abdopublishing.com

Published by Abdo Kids, a division of ABDO, PO Box 398166, Minneapolis, Minnesota 55439.
Copyright © 2017 by Abdo Consulting Group, Inc. International copyrights reserved in all countries.
No part of this book may be reproduced in any form without written permission from the publisher.

Printed in the United States of America, North Mankato, Minnesota.

052016

092016

 THIS BOOK CONTAINS
RECYCLED MATERIALS

Photo Credits: Glow Images, iStock, Shutterstock

Production Contributors: Teddy Borth, Jennie Forsberg, Grace Hansen

Design Contributors: Candice Keimig, Dorothy Toth

Cataloging-in-Publication Data

Names: Murray, Julie, author.

Title: The library / by Julie Murray.

Description: Minneapolis, MN : Abdo Kids, [2017] | Series: My community: places
    | Includes bibliographical references and index.

Identifiers: LCCN 2015959208 | ISBN 9781680805376 (lib. bdg.) |
    ISBN 9781680805932 (ebook) | ISBN 9781680806496 (Read-to-me ebook)

Subjects: LCSH: Libraries--Juvenile literature. | Buildings--Juvenile literature.   Classification: DDC 027--dc23

LC record available at http://lccn.loc.gov/2015959208

Table of Contents

The Library

A library is a special place.

It is filled with books!

Anyone can use the library.

Ava looks at books.

The library is a quiet place.

Max talks **softly**.

The librarians can help you.

They answer your questions.

There are chairs to sit and read. There are tables to work at, too!

There are computers to use.

Lucy looks up **information**.

Nate finds a book.

He wants to take it home.

You can check out books.

Mark uses his library card.

Have you been to a library?

At the Library

books

librarian

computers

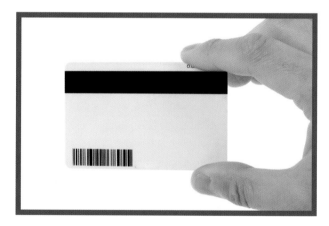

library card

Glossary

information
facts or details about a subject.

soft
in a quiet and gentle way.

Index

abdokids.com

Use this code to log on to abdokids.com and access crafts, games, videos, and more!

Abdo Kids Code:
MTK5376